MW00489371

Paddle Tails

Reflections on people and dogs
who find balance on the water

Maria Christina Schultz

Lisa Chinn Marvashti

See you on the Water!

Maria Schultz

© Maria Christina Schultz, 2016

All rights reserved.

No part of this publication may be reproduced, stored in, or introduced into a retrieval system, or transmitted, in any form, or by any means (electronically, mechanically, by photocopying, recording, or otherwise) without the prior written permission of the authors, except in the quotations embodied in critical articles or reviews.

The scanning, uploading, and distribution of this book via the Internet or via any other means without the permission of the authors is illegal and punishable by law. Please purchase only authorized electronic editions, and do not participate in or encourage electronic piracy of copyrighted materials. Your support of the authors' rights is appreciated.

Published by Maria Christina Schultz
Fredericksburg, Va., USA

mariachristinaschultz.com

ISBN: 978-0692432549

Cover design and book design by Maria Christina Schultz. Cover photo, Garth Riley and Rebecca Randolph.

Photographs by Maria Christina Schultz unless otherwise credited. All photographs are copyrighted and cannot be used or reproduced without written permission from the authors or credited photographers.

Disclaimers:
The purpose of this book is to share the stories of others who have found comfort in paddling with their dogs, and to inspire other dog owners to try similar activities with their dogs. The authors are not veterinarians and are not qualified to offer medical advice. Suggestions made in this book should not replace professional veterinary care. Anyone wishing to participate in a water-related activity should be physically prepared, and seek training advice from a professional trainer or instructor first. The authors and publisher are not liable for any adverse effects or injuries you or your dog may experience from the information contained in this book. Outdoor activities can be risky and should be entered into with caution.

Brands have been named in this book and are present in many of the photographs. These are not necessarily endorsements. Readers should purchase gear that suits their own comfort, needs, and budget.

To Mom, you taught me to listen
and reminded me when I forgot.

Contents

Prologue

It was only 7:30 a.m. and sweat was already dripping down my face as I hauled boards from my car to the beach. Usually one or two students show up ahead of time, and today was no exception. Lisa Godfrey and her brindle boxer, Sadie, were an hour early, and Lisa was bursting with energy.

As I lugged gear from one area to the next, Lisa buzzed around me chatting and laughing. I have to admit, I was trying not to be annoyed, but then she said something that stopped me in my tracks.

"I have to tell you – paddling with Sadie has been the one thing, the *only* thing, I've done for myself that brings me peace. Paddling has saved me." Lisa explained that she had a husband at home with MS and that she was struggling with PTSD.

I was blown away that someone I just met would share such intimate details of her private life. I kept thinking about how Riley, my first Australian shepherd, taught me a valuable life lesson when we started paddling together: It's not how far or how fast you go; it's the company you keep that makes the adventure special.

Now, I was learning that Lisa had found healing on the water with Sadie. I, too, was soaking up some healing as I began to get active on the water with my younger dog, Kona. She was helping me deal with the loss of my mother.

Lisa's revelation (see her story on page 13) planted the seed for this book. I realized I wasn't the only one finding something special with a canine on the water. I started delving deeper, and I found inspirational stories from dog owners across the country.

I have pooled those here reflections in hopes of inspiring others.

– Maria

photo by Norm Shafer

Kisses from Kona

We were having the ultimate summer. Riley, my 5-year-old Australian shepherd, and I had discovered paddleboarding. Because of that board, our bond was stronger than ever.

I'd switched to the sport after a decade of serious rock climbing, which left Riley waiting for me at the base of each climb, sleeping next to me in our tent, and riding in the front seat to every crag. On weekends, we were inseparable.

Life was perfect. Almost.

During the week, while I was at work, I had a nagging feeling. I hated that Riley was alone. I'd long thought about getting a second dog but had put the idea away. I was reluctant to divide my attention, but I believed Riley should have a buddy.

I asked around for advice, starting with my best friend – my mom. She adored dogs and was especially close to Riley. She didn't hold back; she told me I was nuts. Riley wouldn't like sharing my attention, she said. It wasn't the answer I wanted.

I turned next to my dog-trainer friends. They all had more than one dog; the theory being that their canines were happier with pals. After all, dogs are pack animals, and Riley thrives on companionship. My gut said to go for it.

I put the word out. We were looking for another Aussie, one with an easygoing personality like Riley's, an older pup, already housebroken, and preferably female. As luck would have it, a friend knew two excellent breeders, who had just that day put one of their prized show pups up for adoption. She sounded perfect – 4 months old, happy-go-lucky, already trained – not to mention as cute as a button.

My husband, John, and I took Riley to meet the puppy and her breeders at a park in a neutral location in order to give both dogs a fair chance at getting along. As we got out of the car and walked over to the puppy, Riley caught on. He held his chin up, kept his distance, and refused to look at her.

John and I, on the other hand, were amazed by the calm demeanor of the pup. She sat poised and alert, never losing her composure with anything that might normally distract a young puppy. She was gentle and sweet. A friend and professional dog trainer had shared some words of wisdom: "Don't make your decision about a second dog from Riley's reaction; make it on how *you* feel."

Considering Riley's behavior and Mom's advice, I was still hesitant. But looking down at this adorable girl, I felt excited. Something about her tugged at my heart. How could she not grow on Riley? John agreed. She seemed perfect.

On the drive home, we decided to name her "Kona," after the dark coffee we'd enjoyed every morning on a recent trip to Hawaii. Plus, her white and brown markings were like cream and sugar. It wasn't until later we learned that "Kona" in Hawaiian also means a southwesterly winter wind, often bringing strong rain. In other words, "a storm."

Let's just say by the time we got home, the forecast had changed.

Kona pranced through the front door and up the steps of our townhouse, spotted Riley's basket of toys, and — suddenly — she transformed! It was just like the movie *Lilo & Stitch*. Stitch pretends to be a good dog at the pound so Lilo will adopt him. When they get home, he reveals his true identity. He isn't a dog; he's an alien — a very destructive alien.

Kona pulled a Stitch, jumping on every piece of furniture and relieving herself on the carpet and the couch. She also introduced her amazingly loud bark while tearing Riley's toys apart — one by one. John and I just stood there, jaws on the floor.

She tricked us!

Riley took refuge from the storm in the basement, where he stayed. All. Night.

Kona might have been a complete alien, but one thing was clear: She liked me. She couldn't have cared less about Riley and John, but she never took her eyes off of me. She followed me everywhere.

She wore herself out from wrecking the house and fell fast asleep on the couch, so cute and innocent. I sat gently on the opposite end, hoping not to wake her, but I did. She climbed over on top of my chest, gave me a sloppy wet kiss, nuzzled her head under my chin, and fell back asleep.

Over the next several months, Kona tested us in more ways than a blizzard would test Hawaiians.

We hadn't been able to housebreak her, and we were having trouble with obedience. She barked at everything — cars, kids, squirrels…dust. And not just any bark. A high-pitched, nails-on-a-chalkboard type of yelp. She was not at all afraid to use it — in the middle of the night, at the crack of dawn, or while we were trying to watch TV.

Kona was like me — a total tomboy. She excavated more dirt from our tiny backyard than is moved during an entire season of *Gold Rush*. She was a mud magnet, seeking out puddles to roll in, digging, and, yes, eating the brown stuff. She was always sick, often at the vet, and constantly in the bathtub. Through all the barking — and barfing — she never left my side. If there was a mess to be made, Kona proudly made it right next to me.

One afternoon. John and I took both dogs to the river to introduce Kona to the water. As usual, we brought the paddleboard. As soon as we got it water-ready, Riley hopped on, sitting proudly with me, like a king on his throne. This was his territory. But little Kona wanted on, too. Normally quiet, Riley barked and snarled. If looks could kill, poor Kona would have been sent down that river without a paddle — or a human.

I was worried. As ashamed as I am to admit this, I considered taking Kona back to the breeders. Things were getting bad. Riley was upset; I felt like I was betraying the trust of my first "child." John was also agitated. Kona was keeping us up all night, and destroying the house, the furniture, and the car. Even our friends were avoiding us.

I called Mom.

She reminded me she'd been right. Mom loved to do that. If it wasn't working out, according to her maternal wisdom, it wouldn't be fair to Kona – or to us – to keep her.

Before making any decisions, I wanted Mom to meet Kona and see for herself what we had on our hands. Kona was in a particularly difficult mood on the seven-hour drive to Buffalo, New York. She hated the car, and she let us know that by getting sick several times. Would her storm of destruction never end?

We arrived at my sister-in-law's much later than expected, thanks to Kona. Everyone was asleep. We tiptoed into the house, set up Kona's crate, and snuck into the guest bedroom. I had just crawled under the covers and cuddled up with Riley when there it was – the bark! I flew out of the bedroom to stop her before she woke up the house.

I was in tears. I didn't want to give up on this dog, but I couldn't figure her out. I picked her up and took her to the couch, refusing to let her wriggle out of my arms. I sat there with her and cried until she settled down and put her head under my chin.

I remembered the good feeling I'd had the day we met in the park and the night she crawled on top of me at home. I was beginning to realize something.

The problem was not Kona; it was *me*. I was failing this dog.

Of course she would bark, alone in a strange house, while the rest of her pack was asleep in another room. At that moment, I promised her I wouldn't let her go. She would be my dog, and we would make this work. She fell asleep – in my arms – then so did I. When I awoke in the morning, her head was still there, tucked under my chin.

We drove the rest of the way to Niagara Falls to meet Mom. When she walked across the yard to greet Kona, Mom looked more beautiful than ever. And you could feel it – an instant connection.

She picked Kona up like a baby and demanded we snap a picture.

"Oh, Maria, she's just sensitive," Mom said. "She's a tender heart."

Moms are always right. I knew what I needed to do.

I had to give up my guilt about Riley. Because of his jealousy toward Kona, I had been giving Riley more attention than usual. What I finally realized is that Kona needed attention, too. Her barking and misbehavior came from feeling left out.

We began giving the dogs separate training sessions, separate activities, separate attention — and it worked.

Riley and I paddled; Kona and I ran trails and played Frisbee. We took obedience and agility classes. Things got better — a lot better. After nearly a year, Kona was becoming a well-mannered young lady, and I was getting more sloppy wet kisses than ever. Since she never left my side, John even nicknamed her "Shadow."

By now, our little family was in a much better place. Individual activities turned into pack activities, and Riley was softening. He and Kona began chasing each other around the yard in the mornings and running through the woods together in the evenings. The first time I realized they'd started their own routines, I called Mom to tell her the great news: We'd done it!

We had a new problem, though. Kona hated being left behind when I took Riley paddling. Could I paddle with both dogs?

I was writing my first book, *How to SUP With Your PUP*, so I tested my training plan on Kona. I started the same way I had with Riley – in our living room. Kona had a hard time sitting still, but she slowly caught on and we made our way to the water.

She paced on the board and barked – no, we still hadn't gotten rid of that awful bark – more nervous than Riley ever had been. By the end of the summer, though, Kona was comfortable enough to ride with him. We had a few successful short rides as a threesome. Progress!

More elated than ever, I again called Mom. This time, we didn't talk about the dogs. She had some news of her own.

Early that spring, she'd been diagnosed with stage-3 ovarian cancer. While I'd spent the summer training the dogs, she'd been enduring chemo. I began visiting her regularly, and she was even able to come to Virginia to see the dogs in action. But her pain accelerated rapidly. One day I was in Virginia paddling with the dogs; the next day I was in New York at the hospital with Mom.

As winters often do, this one brought a turn for the worse. My mother's health was failing. The chemo wasn't working, and the cancer had spread. I was traveling to New York every other weekend, trying to help her find the right doctors, treatments, and hospitals. She had a constant flurry of medical complications and hardly enough time to dig out.

When a call came from hospice shortly thereafter, I put the dogs in the car and sped to New York. I had been leaving them at home during these treks. But, somehow, this time, I knew I would need them. Kona and Riley gave me the strength I needed to make it to the hospital each morning and the reason I needed to return each night to rest.

One cloudy afternoon, five nights in, I was spent. It was getting harder by the hour to watch Mom fade away. So I took the dogs to a park with a big sledding hill and we wore ourselves out playing Frisbee. Then we sat there, on top of the hill, enjoying the cool spring air – Riley on my left, Kona on my right.

Suddenly, the clouds broke apart and rays of sunlight made their way through in perfect individual beams. My spirituality kicked in, and I felt like I was experiencing a heavenly gift.

Mom died that night.

The death of a mother means the loss of a constant in your life, an anchor. A mother's love transcends distance and time. It's an unceasing love that I felt wherever I was, whatever I was doing. I'd lived 400 miles from Mom for eight years, yet we'd never been closer. We'd become best friends, talking every day, sharing everything.

For months, I struggled. By this time, Riley and Kona were inseparable, and I was grateful for that; we'd been through a lot together. On some level, I believe Riley knew Mom was no longer with us. He'd always been my biggest comfort in hard times, but now that he was sad, too, Kona stepped in.

The "storm" had turned into a rainbow. Kona's presence was bright and affirming.

Now, when I'm cooking or when I'm singing along to the radio, she looks up at me, head tilted. She's listening. If I'm reading on the couch, she curls up with me. She's providing comfort. When we're hiking, she stays close. She's loyal. When I can't find the energy to get outside, Kona barks at me, pushing me. She's motivating. And when I wake up every morning, she gives me kisses. She's loving.

If you stop to think about it, these are the attributes of a mother. A mother's love is a constant, like Kona – my "shadow" – never leaving my side. Even though Mom is no longer with me, I can still feel her love. Kona's kisses remind me.

The healing we've found together is only stronger on the water.

After Mom's death, the dogs and I picked up where we'd left off, paddling as a pack. Having both of them with me was the medicine I needed. I craved it. All I wanted to do, all summer long, was paddle with Riley and Kona. Those outings represented life pared down to two essentials – water, the source of all life, and companionship.

The water is where we connect, build trust, and live in the moment. I forget about the stresses and sadness of life and concentrate on the sound of my paddle pulling us along. And when I look down at my board, the two dogs in tow, I feel safe.

Whatever storms come my way, I now know I can handle them, and I won't be alone. My dogs are with me. And so is my mom.

photo by John Schultz

2
The Boxer Bunch

She was on a white beach when she saw them. The girls with the paddleboards, peeling out past the breakers, standing up in the sea.

She would've been out there, too, if she could have, where the waves turn the ocean to foam, salty spray in her face. But at 19, U.S. Army Records Specialist Lisa Godfrey, away from home for the first time, had a job to do.

Those long sporty boards would resurface in her life more than three decades later but still just in time. When MS and PTSD threw her off course, a paddleboard and her beloved boxers – especially a brindle named Sadie B. – would help her find balance, both on the water and off.

"My dogs are my support system," Lisa said, gazing out the window of the one-story home multiple sclerosis forced her to buy.

Their likenesses, in miniature – Zip, Lacey, Blizzard, and Sadie – trim the pine tree inside the front door. A garland of green winds up the stairs. Cinnamon and carols hang in the room.

One crinkle changes everything in the Chesterfield home, near Virginia's Tidewater region. Treats! Four cropped tails shake like bobble-heads on a bumpy road. Ears everywhere! Eight big eyes on one slim lady with spiky red hair. Even Revy the cat perks up.

Just one thing is missing from this holiday scene: Allen, Lisa's husband of 37 years.

He's in the bedroom, just off the kitchen. Probably watching TV, Lisa says, maybe ESPN or the afternoon news.

Things were different back in 1978 when they met. President Carter had halted production of the neutron bomb, gas was 63 cents a gallon, and the Bee Gees were tearing up disco. In the military, the Women's Army Corps had disbanded, and men and women were living together for the very first time.

Lucky for Lisa.

She was just settling in at Schofield Army Base in Hawaii, working on wrestling her strong Southern roots into something better suited for island life. She hit the beach quick and made friends even quicker. She was clicking with her free-spirit roommate, Lucy, and loving her job.

Lisa had been in sunny Oahu for just a few weeks when she saw him – the tall young supply sergeant shooting hoops with the guys outside the barracks. They met face-to-face in the mess hall.

"In his boldness, he came over and sat down with me," Lisa said of Allen, who showed up at her table with a tray full of French fries and a pair of hot dogs to share.

"He was so nervous he was shaking," she says. "Right, Allen?" she calls over her shoulder into the bedroom. He's watching the Saturday game.

He was a softie, she said, from their very first date – ice cream at Baskin-Robbins. And when she had her wisdom teeth out, after she'd been transferred to Fort Shafter, Allen borrowed a car from a friend and hit Highway H-3 to Honolulu, just to take care of her.

Neither could know how the tables would turn.

They'd dated a year when they gathered before the great King Kamehameha, in the days before rowdy children and ne'er-do-wells forced officials to cordon it off. September sun beamed off the golden-robed statue. Lucy was matron of honor. Allen wore khakis and sported a tie; Lisa a sundress so thin Allen teased that the tourists' cameras might capture more than they'd bargained for.

Allen moved in with Lisa at Shafter and commuted to Schofield. Married life in the land of pineapples and palm trees – a hub of defense and diversity – was heaven. They hung out at home and on Honolulu's sugar-topped beaches. A magical time when their worries were small. Who would trim the weeds? Should they shoo the cats off the stereo?

"We had each other and that's what mattered," Lisa said. "If we argued, we never took it to work."

Three years into the marriage, Lisa began to feel sick. It was the good kind. At 4:36 on a Tuesday afternoon – after a smooth pregnancy and a six-hour labor – she and Allen welcomed Amber, an easygoing baby girl with a headful of hair. She lit up their world.

Lisa and Amber came along, of course, when Allen was transferred to West Germany. By then a civilian, Lisa thrived overseas. The Cold War was winding down, the Berlin Wall was on borrowed time, and this budding young family was moving up in the ranks.

But trouble was lurking.

They'd been in Nuremberg less than a year when Allen suddenly lost vision in one eye. Doctors wrote him a prescription for a 10-hour flight across the Atlantic to be diagnosed in the States. It was optic neuritis — an inflammation of the nerves that send sight signals to the brain — an early sign of MS. A CAT scan confirmed the diagnosis. He was 28.

Multiple sclerosis tears into the brain, causing neurons to misfire, and damaging the pathways that send messages to the body. Scar tissue grows, making it harder and harder for messages to get through. Eventually, they just can't.

Allen endured bouts of neuritis here and there, poor balance, and headaches — and heat did a number on him — but he seemed to be "OK for the longest time," Lisa said, as the military bounced the family from Kansas to Michigan, and finally, back home to Virginia.

Somewhere along the line, MS tightened its grip, forcing Lisa to watch while her military man — her strong basketball player husband, her hero, her love — gave in to a cane, a walker, and worse. By 34, Allen was in a wheelchair. They waged their own private war against the disease, hacking through tangles of treatments and trials, doctors and drugs.

Through it all, while she cared for Amber – and Allen – Lisa was climbing into her car every morning, working full time at Central Michigan University. The schedule was brutal, and it was taking a toll.

But there was something else, too. Something deeper and darker. An invisible enemy launching migraines so strong she'd miss work for days and nightmares so wicked she'd wake up in sweats.

She lost friends. Gained weight. Fell into depression. "I knew I had to do something for myself," Lisa said, "but also for my family."

She reached out to the Veterans Administration, started seeing a counselor. Together, they sifted through the layers of Lisa's past, unearthing the truth, one grain at a time. A fellow officer. A friend of a friend. An assault so brutal her brain had worked hard to forget it.

Her mind had shielded her from acknowledgement of an attack during her first weeks in the Army. But that protection had come at a cost. What she was dealing with now had a name: post-traumatic stress disorder. To put the horror behind her, she would have to relive it – every terrifying second. It was torture.

She turned to her dogs.

Lisa got hooked on the boxer breed – the smooth coats, squared heads, and fierce loyalty – as a girl growing up in central Virginia. Duchess, a birthday surprise from her dad; Shannon, a gift from Allen after they married; Chelsea, the runt of the litter who turned into a swan. She loved them all. The loss of each one hit her harder and harder. She made a decision.

"I was determined that I was never going to be without one again," she said.

And that's the way they became "The Boxer Bunch," as Lisa refers to them on her website and professionally. Blizzard, 1, shamelessly fearless and crazy for tug toys, is (shh!) Allen's favorite. Sadie B., 7, lays claim to her shotgun position in Lisa's SUV. Zip, 8, a homebody, has a thing for bananas. And then there's sweet Lacey, 11.

"I'm so in tune with them. If you listen with your heart, you can hear what they have to say," Lisa said. "I understand my dogs better than I understand people."

Few places is that bond more apparent than in her backyard. Filled with tunnels and jumps, it's a doggie-style Disneyland, a playground of wellness for pups and their people.

Now that Amber is grown, Lisa's boxers are her babies. She plasters their pictures all over Facebook, takes them to the pool, and fills a hope chest with their pictures, ribbons, and other mementos. She bakes them treats – oatmeal bones, banana yummies – from scratch. And, get this…on their birthdays, she takes them to the bakery to pick out a cake.

Lisa might binge on affection from her boxers, but she shares the love, too, opening her backyard and its equipment to her dog-trainer friends. She volunteers with Blue Ridge Boxer Rescue and Caring Canines Dog Therapy of Richmond. She teaches agility at the SPCA and started Read-2-Rover at Fort Lee Community Library. The first of its kind in the Army, the program promotes literacy by bringing the most accepting of listeners to kids who are timid about reading aloud.

If her work with the boxers and her therapist, and the love of her family and friends — with two legs *and* four — helped Lisa deal with the darkness of PTSD, a neighbor's invitation put her healing into high gear.

"I was thankful that Sherry [and her border collie, Willow] said to come paddle," Lisa said. "I was over there every week."

On the calm waters of Woodland Pond, not far from the chaos of Interstate 95, Lisa finds peace. Ringed by luxury homes, it's a long way from that white beach in Hawaii, but it brought back the memory of the girls on the boards from so long ago.

It's Lisa's turn now.

Determined to teach herself how to balance and steer, she'd pack up her paddleboard and practice each week after work. Once she felt comfortable, she invited a guest.

Sadie B. – "Sabel Sirocco Barhopping Baby" – was 6 weeks old when Lisa saw the ad in the paper. She was small enough to fit in one hand, "full of worms," and didn't have papers. But Lisa wasn't leaving without her.

Turns out, Sadie's a natural on a paddleboard, hopping right on that first day, while Lisa and Sherry sat chatting on the dock. Sadie doesn't stand on the board like Lisa does, as they pull their way through the taupe-colored water. Instead, she lies down, nestled on the nose of the B-Ray in her sun-colored lifejacket. Her dark-as-coal eyes, filled with compassion and focus, say it all. She's returning the gift of hope Lisa gave her as a puppy, helping Lisa find balance.

This spring, she and Allen started a new chapter, as they say, welcoming a grandson. Lisa, or "Lela," as baby Drew will call her, officially retired from the Department of Defense and was thinking of floral design as a way to keep her healing on track.

But in a world where change swirls all around us, loved ones become people we never even knew, and life brings us paddleboards, some things remain.

On sunny days, you'll still find Lisa and Sadie B. out on the lake, standing on water. Wednesdays are best, midweek, when humans are scarce and nature's on show – herons, eagles, beavers, and turtles. When everything's quiet and still, and peace can take hold.

"When you step out there on the water, you don't think about anyone else. It's serene," Lisa said. "It's like a dance with your dog."

3
Splash. Shake. Repeat.

Mike Tavares has a few minutes to kill before a big race, but the pro-paddler can't bring himself to sit back and wait. He pulls a pivot turn, tosses the nose of his inflatable onto the dock, and throws a wicked roundhouse, nearly sending his teammate's iPhone into the drink.

He finishes off with a flurry of cross steps, before his best friend, Shredder, jumps in, barking at the board as he leaps on and off. For Mike, who makes a living ripping up rivers, and "Shred Dog," as he's known in the paddling world, life never stands still.

Even their house moves. Together, they chase sun and surf from one coast to the next, covering tens of thousands of miles each year.

"Whether [we travel] 20 minutes or four hours," said Mike, who pilots their 25-foot motorhome, "when we stop, Shredder is ready to go. For these two, "rest" areas mean skateboarding, mountain-biking, Onewheel sessions, and more. But it's paddling that keeps them afloat.

You'd never know now, but when Mike rescued his sidekick – a wiry mix of chow, pit bull, Shih Tzu, and cocker spaniel – from a Tennessee shelter back in 2010, the dog wanted nothing to do with the water.

Not knowing why Shredder was scared, Mike tried something he doesn't typically demonstrate: patience. He bought a canine life vest and spent a year coaxing Shredder into the tide a few feet at a time. Eventually Shred Dog grew gills, and they've been on the go ever since.

"He never stops moving, as soon as he gets on the board," Mike said. "He just can't help himself!"

4

A Casting Friendship

The muscles in her back legs twitch as she hears the drag go off. Something's on the line! She wriggles from her spot on the nose of the kayak, anxious to discover what's been caught.

It's a "look-down" fish, one Ajja can easily see when she peers into the shallow water. The 4-year-old chocolate Lab shakes as Christina Altman coaxes the hook from the fish's mouth and offers it up for the sniffing. Ajja makes a stealthy attempt to snatch the catch, but Christina knows better. She tosses it back into the canal just in time.

It is often said that dogs are reflections of their owners, mirroring each other's personalities and passions. Here on the eastern shore of South Florida, Christina and Ajja are no exception. Both ladies live to fish, and they both look good doing it, complementing each other out on the water.

A few times a week after work, Christina grabs her gear – a Shimano reel and Redbone rod – and tosses it into her white Toyota pickup, with a 13-foot kayak hanging out the back. In an instant, Ajja's in the truck, too.

"She knows," Christina said. "Her head goes out the window, and she gets so excited."

The pair put in wherever they might have some luck – Miami's scenic Biscayne Bay, the Fort Lauderdale Intracoastal Waterway, or the Florida Keys.

"Fishing is a way of life," Christina said.

Her talent caught the eye of *Kayak Angler* in May 2011, when she reeled in the magazine's cover. Bronzed and beautiful, Christina stands waist-high in the water. She's in shades and a bright blue bikini, with a smile wider than the 40-inch snook she's showing off for the camera.

On the water with Ajja, though, the Lab steals the show. Fellow fishermen and passengers from tour boats like the Jungle Queen point and wave at Christina and her four-legged first mate.

None of it rattles Christina. Born in Kingston, Jamaica, she dropped her first line when she was 6, learning to fish on her father's small orange and white boat. When she was 7, they moved to South Florida, where he bought a sailboat. The family spent weekends anchored to islands in the Keys or the Bay, soaking in sun and, most importantly, fishing.

Back then, she'd been a cat person, fine with the no-fuss lifestyle of caring for felines: Bringle, Domino, Blackie, and now Simon, their 15-year-old snowshoe cat. Purring and clawing were one thing. Dogs were a whole different ball of yarn.

Troy, Christina's husband, was the one who had grown up with dogs — Labs, hounds, and rotties. So when the bartender at a pub where he often has lunch mentioned his Labrador's 2-week-old litter, Troy rushed over to pick out the right pup. In the weeks that passed before they could bring home their puppy, Christina acquired three things: lots of potty-training pads, the perfect brand puppy chow, and worry.

As a South Florida police officer for nearly two decades, she pulls the long shifts, working 10-hour days in a patrol car. The station on the state's southern tip doesn't see lots of crime, but there's always someone in need of help. What if owning a dog, especially an energetic Lab, wouldn't work with her schedule?

But when Christina saw 6-week-old Ajja for the first time, her heart melted. The wobbly little puppy with green eyes would come home two weeks later and become the center of her world. "She's been my baby ever since," Christina said of Ajja, now 4. "The princess."

Ajja jumped right into a routine, running down to the dock on the saltwater canal behind their home, palling around with Tootsie, the other chocolate Lab on the block, and hanging out with Christina and Troy wherever they went.

Ajja was about the same age (in dog years) as Christina was when she took her first fishing-boat voyage. It was New Year's Day, chilly and crisp. Christina and Troy hauled their white Action Craft Flats fishing boat out into Biscayne Bay in hopes of catching their favorite – snapper – for dinner. Little did they know how much Ajja would learn on that trip or how quickly she'd fall in love with the sport.

Like most Labs who'll eat just about anything, Ajja learned she preferred the flavor of fish – trout, snapper, or whatever wiggles – to the dog food Christina buys her. An hour into that first trip, Christina caught Ajja trying to gnaw her way through a bag of frozen shrimp! "If I don't keep an eye on her, she'll eat all the baitfish!"

The second thing Ajja learned: What happens when a fish is on the line. "The first time she heard the drag go off, her ears perked up and her eyes got huge," Christina said. "When I started bringing one in, she wiggled and shook, watching to see what was happening. She quickly learned what everything meant." After that, Ajja was hooked. Whenever she hears a drag zip, she runs over to see what's on the line.

But when they fish from the boat, "we race from spot to spot trying to find the next catch," Christina said. She wanted to try something different with Ajja, something more relaxing. "In a kayak, life slows down; we can go at our own pace."

But there was a problem. Ajja, full-grown, couldn't fit comfortably in the watercraft. Christina found this unacceptable and started shopping for a new one. One with a nice flat spot on the nose for her 83-pound copilot.

She bought a new 13-foot mango-colored kayak and tossed in a patio cushion to make Ajja's seat comfy. Next, Christina selected a life jacket for her girl, a bright yellow one to coordinate with the kayak and her PFD! It started a pattern – every piece of gear Christina considers, she keeps Ajja in mind. A versatile fisherman, Christina also casts from a stand up paddleboard. When her board wouldn't accommodate both fishing gear and Ajja, she traded it in for a dog-friendly model. Then she customized it with a PUP Deck for Ajja to sit on up at the nose.

From the back seat of her tandem kayak, with Ajja in the front looking over the bow, Christina paddles them through Florida's inland waterways, where they work together to catch fish. Christina watches for the head tilt; she can always tell when Ajja spots a potential catch. On each trip, she makes a point to steer them onto a beach or into a cove, where Ajja can work on her own angling skills.

She paces in the shallow water, back and forth, ears cocking, tail wagging, head darting in and out of the water. She's mesmerized, watching for anything that moves. When Ajja sees a fish she might be able to catch, she pounces, corrals the fish into a corner, and pounces again. Mullets are her favorite. The small baitfish swim in close and are easy to see – the perfect catch for a fishing dog and her adoring owner.

"As long as she's fishing, she's happy," said Christina, who feeds off Ajja's energy.

For Christina, it's about tranquility and slowing down, a chance to unwind. No patrol car. No paperwork. No bad guys. For Ajja, it's time spent with her best girlfriend, and the thrill of the catch.

"I try to involve her in everything I do, especially paddling" Christina said. "She loves the water so much, I just can't leave her behind."

5
She's All Ears

It was a typical hot Nevada day when Maria Bartels and boyfriend Duane headed out to Red Rock Canyon to climb. She had no way of knowing that her favorite crag – and two words she'd hear as she entered the park – would change her outlook on life. "Free dog!"

Maria whirled around to see two young siblings holding a battered dog, barely bigger than a baby bunny. They'd watched a man in a pickup toss her out the window, then speed away, leaving them all in the red desert dust.

For months, Maria had been feeling down, slow to get out of bed. Depression had made it difficult for her to care for herself, much less a pet. But how could she just walk away? She tucked the pint-sized pup – all five pounds of her – into her climbing bag and drove home to Las Vegas.

The dog was malnourished, dehydrated, and riddled with skin irritations. But, those ears. Oh, those big ears. Maria named her Coco, after Calico Basin, her favorite place in Red Rock.

They'd spend the next several months in and out of the vet, Coco's sheen getting brighter each day, along with Maria's mood. Caring for the Chihuahua-dachshund mix was helping her put things in perspective and let go of the pain from the past several years.

She had a reason now to get out of bed…and a reason to take Coco to work with her. A paddleboard instructor, Maria helps tourists navigate the Colorado River by SUP. That first day on the job together, Coco leaped onto Maria's giant stand up paddleboard, ears perked, and everything fell into place.

"Paddling with Coco has given me a deeper appreciation for life and companionship," Maria said. "When we paddle, I feel like nothing can stop us."

6

A Boy Named Finnigin

"Line of scrimmage," Christine Cancian calls to her brood.

Abbygael, Molly, and Brady spread out across the field. Finnigin lines up in front of Brighton, staring through his curly blond locks into Brighton's blue eyes.

"Ready, hit!" Brighton yells.

The family's star athlete, Brighton fakes left and sprints down the field to the right. Finnigin weaves between him and the quarterback, trying to intercept the ball. But he's not fast enough.

"Score!" Brighton calls. He lands the winning touchdown, and everyone high fives. "Nice try, Fin. Maybe next time."

For some homeschoolers, recess might mark the end of a long day of learning, but for this party of five, it's just the beginning. Their mother, Christine, has her work cut out for her, planning daily lessons and adventures for Abbygael, 15; Molly, 13; Brady, 11; Brighton, 9; and, of course, Finnigin, who's 5.

A proud member of this big Irish family, Fin's a goldendoodle – half golden retriever, half poodle – who believes, truly believes, he's one of the siblings. The Pinocchio-like tale weaves its way through the family's every facet, human and canine, making it difficult to tell who's teaching whom.

It all started one chilly November afternoon. Christine and husband Brian had been kicking around the idea of getting a dog for Christmas. They were just going to "look" at a litter of goldendoodles.

The puppies wouldn't be old enough to bring home for the big day.

But when they got to the breeder's farm, they found a surprise: a second, older litter, with seven adorable puppies, all ready for homes. As Abbygael, Molly, Brady, and Brighton doted on the little balls of fur, the puppies soaked up the attention. One in particular was falling in love with the Cancian crew. While his litter mates got sidetracked, traipsing out into the yard to sniff and explore, he stayed behind, circling the Cancian children again and again.

Christine saw the connection, and she made a decision – Christmas would come early.

When they all piled back into the minivan to go home, they had one extra passenger. The kids scrunched together, nudging aside paddles and strewn-about gear to make room.

Their newest addition would need a name – Irish like the rest of the kids, short enough for young Brighton to pronounce, and fitting for the pup's fun personality. Christine tossed out ideas, and one stuck: Finnigin Barley Cancian. "Fin" for short.

With such a large clan, good manners were a must for Fin, and naturally, training would be a family affair. Once a week for six weeks, they all crammed into the car – parents, children, and pet – and made their way to obedience class. Learning the same commands at the same time would make training – and domestic life – a little easier for everyone.

"It was also a great out-of-the-classroom learning opportunity for the kids," Christine said.

The team approach worked! Fin slipped seamlessly into the family's outdoor adventures and homeschooling routine – math, science, English, and history in the mornings; outdoor learning in the afternoons. While Fin is present for nearly all lessons, the children will tell you, he sleeps through most of them.

By snack time, though, he's always wide awake.

All the learning makes everyone hungry, especially Fin, so Molly plunks five glasses onto the counter and pulls out the blender. Fin follows her, hoping for handouts. Apple cakes are his weakness, and the family learned the hard way that these delicacies need to cool on the very top shelf. Today, Molly, an avid reader and artist, is making everyone's favorite snack, peanut butter and banana milkshakes. The kids crowd around the counter, and Fin paces and pants, anxious for his share. No one ever said he's not spoiled.

Next on the schedule is music, and everyone gathers in the living room for Brady's recital. He settles in on the sofa to play *Dan O'Keefe's Slide* on his button box accordion, and Fin hops up, too, scooching in close. As Brady works the instrument's bellows and keys, Fin tunes in, turning the number into a duet. He howls along, hitting all the right notes…most of the time.

The backyard pool is also a classroom, and this evening Christine is teaching wet exits. An ACA-certified kayak and SUP instructor, she preaches the importance of learning self-rescue techniques. Fin waits patiently, watching the others learn how to safely get out of a flipped kayak. With each successful attempt, Fin's confidence grows. He knows he can do this, too.

Unprompted, he leaps off the deck into the pool, shimmies his way into the kayak's cockpit, and reaches over the gunnel to propel himself through the water. But something is off; his technique looks different. He can't hold the paddle — no thumbs! Everyone laughs and reassures him. It's OK; they're just proud that he tried.

When classes are completed, there's finally a chance for some down time. And no one takes down time more seriously than Fin. Most evenings, he races into the living room before anyone else grabs his favorite armchair. But this night, as he wags his way into the room, he hears a loud noise.

Thunder!

Abbygael!

He darts upstairs to find her, along with the reassurance he needs. She's in her room practicing the fiddle but drops it to comfort her pal. The oldest of the four Cancian kids, Abbygael's the one Fin trusts most. It's an incredible bond; Fin turns to her when he's had a bad day or when there's something scary on his schedule, like a visit to the vet.

Don't even get him started on going to the groomer. When Christine takes him in for a wash and a trim, the staff keeps him distracted, while she sneaks out the front like a mom leaving a toddler at daycare.

The Cancian calendar is packed with events and activities, but no curriculum's complete without field trips, and this family takes them all year. Swimming in lakes, hiking in parks, sledding on snow-covered slopes, and hiking mountain trails are all chances to explore nature and learn to respect the outdoors. And these activities are not just for the two-legged members of the family.

"Everyone always likes to bring Fin along. We tend to feel bad when we don't," Christine said. "It's an all-around win for everyone."

There's just one yearly adventure Fin doesn't get to enjoy – the Vermont family ski trip. This is a complete and total bummer for Fin, who has to spend the week with "Grandma Luskin," Christine's mom. Seeing his human siblings leave without him gets him down. He sulks and refuses to eat his kibbles. To combat his blues, the kids had an idea – daily Skype sessions.

Their pixelated faces a little shaky on the screen, their voices a little off-time, they fill Fin in on what they've been doing and tell him how much they miss him. Fin talks to them, too, in his own way – sniffing the monitor and howling.

Of all the fun things this family does, paddleboarding's become the favorite. Once a week in the summer, when the fountain's full-throttle, spewing bursts of bubbly water into the air, Christine and the kids frequent nearby Coe Lake, Finnigin in tow.

The first time they took him to the picturesque park, Christine had a feeling he'd take to the sport. Big sister Abbygael's old life jacket was a perfect fit for the shaggy 65-pounder. All suited up, Fin

looked across the manicured lawns, past the wooden gazebo, and he spotted Abbygael and Molly on the other side of the lake. He glanced back at Christine, and the poodle part of his brain clicked. He jumped on the board. He sat. Then stood. Then sat again, unsure what to do. Christine kneeled beside him, staying close in case Fin bailed.

"Way to go, Finny!" Abbygael shouted her encouragement across the water. A few words from his consummate comforter were just what he needed. He relaxed, lay down, and hung four paws off the rail.

Christine had an "aha" moment. The special bond between Abbygael and Fin could help reinforce a lesson on trust.

"Finnigin needs to trust the kids to not put him in harm's way," she said, "and the kids need to trust Finnigin not to goof around and knock them off the board."

Day two turned out a lot better. With Abbygael at the helm, Fin's confidence soared. Abbygael glowed as he sat at her feet, completely at ease on the board and keeping a close eye on the rest of the kids.

It's hard to say who was more thrilled with the turn of events. Molly, Brady, and Brighton knew Fin would now get to join them on paddling trips. Fin knew it, too, they think. Since then, his dark soulful eyes light up when he sees someone pulling a paddleboard from the garage.

Not that things always go smoothly.

During one afternoon paddle, Fin had just zeroed in on a fat flock of ducks when one decided to fly off, lighting a spark in the retriever part of Fin's brain. He shot off the board and straight toward the flock. All the squawking and screeching alerted the park rangers, who came out to investigate. They reminded Christine of leash laws, as she quickly got Fin back in control. While no ducks were harmed that day, lessons were learned.

"It taught the kids that situations can be unpredictable when you include a dog," Christine said. "You have to be able to make quick calls."

While they love all outdoor activities, she and her brood agree that there's something special about paddling. Adding Fin to the mix makes the sport feel balanced in more ways than one and creates new challenges to conquer on the water.

"When you climb, it's just you mastering the rock; but when you paddle, there's a centeredness and soul-building peace that takes place within nature and all its beauty," Christine said. "It's just another way for Finnigin to spend time with us in the adventure of life."

photo by Werner Pirker

7
Weightless

So what if he was "a little afraid" of dogs? He was in love. "My girlfriend always wanted one, so I said 'OK.'" Those are the words of Werner Pirker, a pushover for lovely Simona. Newfoundlands, with their massive size and thick drool, aren't exactly starter dogs. But Werner and Simona were determined to make it work.

Pauli was just 2 months old when they got him, a fur ball that mushroomed – 10 pounds per month – into a hulking mass. When he reached his adult weight of 165 pounds, weighing in more than Werner, the family had two problems.

First, they live in Padova, Italy, where the streets, cars, and fenced-in backyards are tiny. How would they keep their gentle giant active?

Second, they had to be careful with Pauli's joints. He had grown too fast and developed osteochondrosis; high-impact sports like running, and agility would be off limits. And "playing with a ball was just too simple," Werner told *Newfoundland Magazine* in March 2015. That is when he "discovered those strange surfing boards with long paddles," Werner said.

Newfies love to swim; the breed has a reputation for rescuing overboard sailors. Plus, they live just a stone's throw from Venice and the beach. Perfetto! Nearly a year would come and go before they'd get their hands on a board that could hold both of them. But once they found the 40-inch wide inflatable and Werner got Pauli used to it by feeding him on it, there was no turning back.

Werner has posted more than 100 YouTube videos of the duo's excursions – Pauli combing beaches and snowcaps with Werner, and waltzing weightless with him in the water. "Doing all this activity with Pauli helps me to relax and forget daily problems," Werner said. "It's freedom."

8
Healing Waters

Eleventh Street spits all manner of traffic onto New York's Pulaski Bridge. Trucks spew exhaust and debris across six lanes of asphalt. Commuters honk and huff. Even cyclists, with their eco-friendly attitudes, shout at each other to get out of the way.

Below, Newtown Creek slogs its way between Brooklyn and Queens, three and half miles of liquid pollution. A layer of sludge – from graffiti-scrawled factories and dusty coal yards – covers the bottom.

On a sun-soaked April morning, Jens Rasmussen and Kimberly Faith Hickman slide a green canoe into the water they're working to heal. By all accounts, they shouldn't be out here, but for this pair of thespians and their two rescued pit bulls – Gertie and Millie – "no" isn't part of the script. Gliding silently past the New York City skyline, the foursome appears peaceful and whole.

Back at the North Brooklyn Boat Club, where they put in, Gertie's wheels wait. The contraption is a stark reminder that the paths of living species – like waterways – do not always follow the expected course.

At home, Gertie races Millie up and down the steep wooden stairs. But a walk through the city for a dog with three legs is different. The rolling rig of metal and canvas helps compensate for Gertie's missing limb and adds support where she carries most of her weight.

"There's a reason you don't see front amputees out and about," said Jens, who knows little about what happened to Gertie in October 2012, when Hurricane Sandy tore onto the East Coast. In its wake, the category-3 storm left a $65 billion tab and hundreds of thousands of homeless people and pets. In the scramble that followed, animal lovers were eager to help, but amputee pit bulls weren't on most wish lists. Gertie got lucky.

But let's go back to this family's opening act.

Winter 2006. Columbus, Georgia. *Romeo and Juliet* lit up the marquee at Springer Opera House, where hunky young actor Jens was taking cues from fiery director and choreographer Kimberly. The Shakespearean romance crept offstage spawning a modern-day love story with its own twists and turns.

Jens grew up in rural Wisconsin; Kimberly four states below in the "Heart of Dixie."

He learned to live off the land and play on the water, swimming, windsurfing, and competitive crewing where the north-rolling Fox River meets Lake Winnebago. A canoe instructor and Maine guide, his survival skills have been featured by *The New York Times* and CBS News.

Kimberly grew up in a family-centric Alabama suburb into all things artistic. She was a toddler when she discovered *Annie* — and a bit of herself in those magical girls singing and dancing onstage — and fell in love with the theater. A high-school reading of the Tony- and Pulitzer-praised *Angels in America* convinced her there was no other way.

Three years after meeting, they were married, in front of the surging white waters of the Chattahoochee River. Kimberly wore a knee-length lace gown, collecting flowers from each of her best friends; her mother sealing the bunch with a paisley-print bow. Jens, in a breezy-cool linen suit, built a fire from flint and passed the flame to each guest until the crowd glowed. Then, the couple hopped on a bike and pedaled away, a trail of tin cans clanking behind them.

Kimberly's house in Columbus worked great for a while, but Jens' third-floor apartment near the thick of New York City theater was calling. Unassuming yet spacious, it's a rent-controlled dinosaur on Brooklyn's north end. A hidden conveyor belt in the bedroom and a pair of giant hinged doors hint at its former life as a potato chip factory. A stairway leads to the roof and a wide-open NYC view.

But even as newlyweds, this couple didn't spend much time at home.

Kimberly plunged into Jens' on-the-go lifestyle, exploring the water and woods. When they weren't boating or camping, they'd flash past each other on the way to auditions, rehearsals, parties, premieres. They work all over the country, often separately – Jens in front of the curtain, Kimberly behind it – with stars like Sarah Jessica Parker and Alicia Silverstone.

But, while they were making a life for themselves and building their résumés in the Big Apple, something was missing. Jens had been busy for months in Georgia, Ohio, and North Carolina. When he got ready to leave once again, this time to work on a show in Washington, D.C., Kimberly made a decision.

"I just sort of hit a limit," she said. "It seemed silly to me to be home and not have a dog."

The Samoyed and German shepherd she'd grown up adoring, the chow mix she'd rescued in college, the dachshund-Chihuahua she'd shared with her ex – canines had stolen her heart. She didn't feel whole without a dog in her life.

"I love animals so much," she said. "I enjoy dogs, the activities you can do with them, how they can get you out of your house."

While Jens worried a dog would cramp their lifestyle and possibly curtail their careers, Kimberly was confident they could make it work. She knew the ticket: a rescue dog. Any shape. Any shade. Any breed. Almost.

"I knew I did not want a pit bull," Kimberly said. "I'd bought into all the stereotypes."

The leaves were just starting to turn the day they grabbed their jackets – and a leash, just in case – hopscotching subways to the ASPCA on the Upper East Side. Each dog had a story – born in a puppy mill, hit by a car, terrified of men. Kimberly would've taken them all if she could've, but one in particular made her mark.

"She came up and peed right by my leg," she said of Millie. "We knew she was the one."

At 3 months, Millie had lived her whole life in a shelter. Her mother had been picked up wandering the streets of the Bronx, about to give birth to a litter of five. The puppy was adorable, Jens said, "a little black roly-poly." There was only one problem. She was a pit bull.

Stories raced through Kimberly's mind. Longtime family pets biting toddlers, attacking innocent dogs. Apartments – even some *countries* – ban pit bulls completely. In the U.S., thousands are euthanized each day.

The folks at the shelter tried to put her at ease. Pit bulls, they assured her, are not inherently mean. Depending on how they are raised, they can be as gentle as any other breed. The folks at the shelter were wasting their time. Kimberly had fallen in love.

Not that Millie's playful puppy teeth, pointy as pins, didn't cause a few freak-out moments early on. As they spent time together, though, Kimberly let down her guard and the family found its new fit, Millie digging deep into Kimberly and Jens' hearts.

They took her to obedience class, for long walks at the dog park, and hiking and camping on weekends, but they were itching to get her into the canoe. They started at home, teaching her to climb in and out of the hull, gradually working their way to the water.

Mischievous, loving, and wise, Millie wasn't slowing them down. She was revving them up, pushing them out of the apartment and into the outdoors even more. Most of all, though, she was teaching Kimberly something important: She'd been wrong about pit bulls.

No wonder she was drawn to that one at the dog park, the white one with the cappuccino-colored spots and one leg wrapped in a scarf. While Millie sniffed out the stranger, Kimberly talked to the owners.

Weeks before, Sandy's 74-mile-per-hour winds had dumped the Atlantic onto the East Coast, causing mandatory evacuations in New York and New Jersey. When Jens, Kimberly, and Millie came home, their rooftop garden – the one Kimberly had so carefully planted with wildflowers – was gone. They were fortunate. Thousands of people and pets had no homes to come back to at all.

They were monitoring the storm and its fallout online, the couple at the park told Kimberly, when a picture popped up on Facebook. It was Gertie.

She'd been picked up in East New York, an area known for pit bull fighting. She was limping along, her right front leg withered, dragging, and bloody. She'd been placed on a much-too-long list of unclaimed dogs that were scheduled to be euthanized. The post was one last attempt to save them. For Gertie, it worked.

The couple had seen something special in her off-kilter eyes, her splotchy pink nose. They'd taken her in, and, after several opinions, made a painful decision. Her surgery was scheduled for the following week.

Next time Jens saw Gertie, her scarf was gone. So was her leg. The surgery had been a success, but there was a new problem. Her owners were being transferred to Canada, where breed-specific laws ban pit bulls in some regions. Gertie was about to be homeless again.

Kimberly got a text: *I'm at the dog park. Do you want to take her?* Her response took all of two seconds. They'd foster Gertie, give her a place to stay. Just for a while. Just until they could find her a good home.

They did *try* to find her a forever family. Really, they did. But meeting potential adopters only made them realize Gertie already had a home — with them.

Turns out, a missing leg was just the beginning for Gertie. She had a heart murmur, incontinence, and a mass cell tumor that required surgery – way more than some would be willing to tackle. But Kimberly and Jens were on board, committed to giving their dogs the best possible life.

When Kimberly shared their story on the set of *The Assembled Parties*, it was Broadway actress Judith Light – from the hit '80s sitcom *Who's the Boss* – who spoke up. She suggested they look into animal prosthetics.

That search came up empty – Gertie's surgery had made an artificial limb infeasible – but it did lead to an answer: Eddie's Wheels for Pets. The Massachusetts-based company makes custom carts, specially measured for all sorts of animals.

Getting the wheels was one thing. Getting Gertie used to them was another. She tipped over, ran into things, tripped, and got tired. Months of practice – in the apartment, on the sidewalk, with a leash – led to the ultimate challenge, learning to walk with her wheels beside Millie. Patience, persistence, and plenty of dog treats paid off.

The wheels changed their lives.

Now that they could make the short trek from their apartment to the boat club in style, they set a new goal: a family outing in the canoe, just the four of them – Jens, Kimberly, and their two 50-pound pits.

"I'm lucky," Jens said. "In an 18-foot canoe, 100 pounds is actually an asset … as long as [the girls] sit still."

That brings us back to the current scene: a late-morning paddle on Newtown Creek.

The sun is working its magic, scraping the edge off the chill in the air. At the boat club, Millie climbs out of the canoe and onto the floating dock, four feet fluttering up a wooden stepladder to land. Jens hoists Gertie up after, and she makes her way to her wheels.

The apartment's just blocks away, but with Gertie, the walk takes awhile. It isn't her legs that slow them down; it's the attention. Today, she turns the heads of a group that has gathered at a bus stop. It isn't unusual. Diners rush out of restaurants. Children ask questions.

"It does seem to happen with some frequency," Jens said. "I'm remembering one young girl in a wheelchair who was really excited to meet Gertie."

This morning, though, they're in a hurry. Jens has a meeting at Google on Ninth. At the apartment, he quickly changes and skims by a vase of pink roses, a closing-night gift from actress Annie Golden (think: *Orange Is the New Black*), his *Underland* co-star.

The meeting is about the environment, including Newtown Creek. Once one of the country's most polluted bodies of water, it was named a Superfund Site, slated by the government for cleanup, in 2009. The following year, Jens co-founded the North Brooklyn Boat Club, promoting stewardship and recreation on the creek and the salty East River it feeds. He's determined to help fellow New Yorkers wring what they can from the water around them.

And it's working.

The water is recuperating. Egrets, osprey, and oysters have returned. Gertie is healing, too, happy to chase after squirrels and christen as many lampposts and street signs as possible.

This family of four, with all its flaws and flourishes, has found a personal playground in an unlikely place.

"There is nowhere in New York City where you can get farther from the crowd than on the waterways," Jens said. "There's something, especially here, about paddling surrounded by skyscrapers that puts things in perspective. You're in a little boat in this big, powerful, intimidating city. It puts the focus where it should be."

photo by Tram Bui

9
Lilo & Rosie

Los Gatos, California. Three sisters, two Siberian huskies, and a cat empty out of an SUV.

The Lake Vasona rental manager: "Ever been on a paddleboard before?"

"Nope!"

"And are all these animals going with you?"

"Yep!"

"The cat, too?"

"Yep!"

"Ooookaaaay," says the manager hesitantly, as he rings up the order for three boards. "Well, at least let me help you carry these down to the water."

The sisters – Thi, Thoa, and Tram Bui – may not be the most experienced paddlers on the water, but they know something others may not: together, anything's possible. Even paddleboarding with a cat who acts more like a dog and two dogs bred to hate water.

For the sisters, ages 19 to 22, who still live together with their mother, animals have always been a big part of their lives. Their San Jose home is a revolving door of rescues, fosters, and strays – everything from bunnies to birds. Permanent residents are Lilo and Infinity, their two red Siberian huskies, sisters from the same litter. While the Bui sisters love dogs, their passion is helping feral cats.

So a coworker of one of the sisters knew exactly where to take the 3-week-old kitten she found on the street, abandoned by her mother.

The cat's eyes were still closed, and she was so lethargic and weak they worried she wouldn't make it through the first night. Thoa, Thi, and Tram tried again and again to feed her, but she refused. They were concerned about malnutrition and dehydration, but they knew she needed something more – the warmth of a mother's fur.

As Lilo, the excitable one, paced around the kitten's crate, Thoa had an idea. It was risky, but it was their last hope to get the kitten to feed.

One of the closest descendants of their wolf ancestors, Siberian huskies are known for their high prey drive. And Lilo and Infinity have plenty of that drive. Were they crazy to pair the canine with the cat?

All three girls huddled in close, on guard in case something went wrong. They opened the crate and held their breath. Lilo lay down in front and the kitten clumsily climbed onto her head and settled between the dog's big pointy ears. The husky's mouth opened but no teeth were shown – just a big gentle tongue that licked the tiny animal clean.

The kitten spent the night nestled into Lilo's thick double coat. In the early morning hours, she accepted the bottle from Thoa and started feeding. The kitten would need round-the-clock care, but the hard part was behind them.

The next day, she opened her eyes – to an unlikely mother and a forever home. The girls named her Rosie. Infinity accepted Lilo's choice to see Rosie as a pup and not as a snack, and she got on board too.

The first time Thoa separated them to take Rosie to the vet, both animals cried and howled until they were reunited. So the girls did what anyone else would do: They bought Rosie a collar and a leash. On daily walks, bike rides, and car trips, and when they play fetch in the park, Rosie is just one of the dogs.

For the huskies, a prey drive isn't the only instinct they've managed to suppress. Like cats, they have a natural aversion to water.

Yet, here they all are. Lilo and Rosie sit together on the nose of Thi's board out in Lake Vasona.

They all stay side by side on the boards. Tram has the camera, and Thoa paddles with Infinity. Not a scene you see every day, but for this pack, it's business as usual.

"With paddleboarding, I felt a sense of accomplishment," Thoa said. "This is something I can do as exercise with all of our pets." And, as if a tighter bond was needed, she added, "Going on adventures with our animals just brings us even closer together."

10
One Fit Family

He shares his adventures with thousands on Instagram, Twitter, and Facebook. He even has his own blog, *The World According to Garth Riley*. But this popular pooch has a private side, too. There's a secret behind his action-packed life, and the health and happiness it's brought to his family.

Garth Riley was born August 8, 2007. The same day, Rebecca Randolph learned her dog, Jake, was dying of cancer. Garth Riley and Rebecca wouldn't meet for more than a year, as she worked through the loss of her beloved black Lab. During that time, she would read a book that would change both of their lives.

Now an attorney near Richmond, Virginia, Rebecca worked as a paralegal as she inched her way toward a law degree. Being chained to her desk for years had taken a toll. Only in her 40s, she felt out of shape, lethargic, and old. Husband Andrew Scarborough, a cross-country athlete in high school, found himself in the same situation.

The loss of Jake, a black ball of fire that became the light of their lives, made things even worse. After he died, Rebecca read *Merle's Door* by Ted Kerasote. The tale, about a dog whose owner allowed him to come and go as he pleased – and what having his freedom meant to him – touched her.

"It made me think a lot about the life a typical dog leads, spending a lot of time at home alone, not experiencing much beyond his own house and yard," Rebecca said. "I wanted to make sure that our next dog led the most enriched and interesting life possible."

She couldn't bear the thought of opening herself up to that kind of heartbreak again right away, but when she felt stronger, she promised herself, she'd make it her mission. A month would go by. Then two and three. It would be almost a year, until finally, one rainy October morning, she and Andrew knew they were ready.

They headed south on the four-hour drive to North Carolina's Outer Banks, the cottage where they used to take Jake, the beach where he used to play. They scattered his ashes there, on the sand, and said their goodbyes.

By the end of the weekend, Rebecca had contacted a King George County Lab breeder. She happened to have a young yellow male who had proven to be a little too short for the show ring, but he was a good, healthy dog. They should come take a look.

Enter Garth Riley.

It was love at first sight. Big on cuddles and kisses, Garth Riley couldn't get close enough to his new owner. Rebecca ate it all up and started making good on her promise. She signed him up for obedience lessons and Dog Scouts of America. Garth Riley became a Canine Good Citizen and a therapy dog. They went hiking, played ball, and walked in the park.

Then came vacation. Along with her stuff and Andrew's, Rebecca packed a crate, a bowl, and some toys. She brought food, treats, and leashes. She lugged along Garth Riley's life jacket, skateboard, and Doggles (doggie sunglasses, for the uninitiated). Their annual trip to the Florida Keys was going to be fun. It was also going to be a turning point.

The summer before, Rebecca had watched a woman slide her paddleboard into the ocean, coax her big brown dog onboard, too, and use two strong arms to pull them both through the sea.

"It looked like so much fun," said Rebecca, reminiscing about childhood days on the family boat and her love for the water.

But she was nervous. She'd gained weight. Lost strength and stamina. She felt she looked nothing like the athletic paddleboarder in her memory. Still, there was Garth Riley. And her promise.

He was there, of course, along with Andrew, cheering her on from the dock as she teetered on that ultra-wide board for beginners, sunshine flickering on the rippled peaks of the water. But Rebecca soon found her sea legs, and a teenager's comment – "You rocked that board!" – sealed the deal. She was hooked.

She was back at it the next day. But this time, she wasn't alone.

"After breakfast, we went to Lazy Dog at Hurricane Hole Marina, and I learned to stand up paddleboard!" Garth Riley blogged. *"At first it was a little scary, but I'll do pretty much anything as long as my mom is there with me. We paddled around the marina for a while, and I got more comfortable, so I lay down with my tail hanging in the water. Mom said it was awesome being able to paddle with me!"*

Rebecca had found a low-impact sport the whole family – she, Andrew, and Garth Riley – could enjoy together. They came back again and again, paddling the turquoise waters of the Florida Bay each day of vacation.

"My favorite Keys activity:" Garth Riley tweeted during the trip, *"SUPing the backcountry w/my mom & dad!"*

Rebecca spent the long nights of winter dreaming of gliding across the water, like she had in a sailboat as a child and on a windsurfer as a teen. So when she learned that SUP lessons were headed to her area in spring, she signed up.

As they worked on balance and polished their techniques, their confidence grew. Rebecca saw each goal she met as a challenge to do more. Together, they took eco tours, group paddles, and advanced lessons. They rented boards weekly and spent long weekends exploring the historic James River. They could not get enough.

"We had such a wonderful time SUPing yesterday!" Garth Riley posted on Facebook. *"I made some new friends!"*

As their social and recreational lives flourished, so did their health. Rebecca and Andrew felt lighter and happier. They had more energy, less stress. They were on a roll. Then Rebecca did something she hadn't done for more than 25 years. She signed up for a 5K. She wasn't sure she was ready, but she had a motive.

"I wanted more stamina for paddling," she said. "So I gave it a try."

During the six months that followed, as her life changed, becoming a blur of running and paddling, so did Rebecca, toning her arms, whittling her waistline, shedding 25 pounds!

"I feel so much younger than I did 10 years ago. I have the energy to do all the cool things I want," said Rebecca, reaching under the picnic table to pet Garth Riley before a paddle on scenic Swift Creek. "It's like I'm back to my old self, before I started feeling like I was too old and limited to do fun things."

When Rebecca ran her first half-marathon, Garth Riley couldn't have been prouder. *"Amazing what my momma has accomplished in the last year!"* he posted on Instagram with a photo of Rebecca's ribbon. *"She added a new medal to her collection today!"*

She dragged Andrew along, too, drawing him back into running. "I can't believe how much I missed it," he said. "It clears my head." At 51, he's setting new personal bests, winning first-place medals in his age group, and at last count, had lost 17 pounds.

Garth Riley is a much tougher sell, said Rebecca. He's devoted to her, to Andrew, and to their active lifestyle, but she cannot convince him to run. The catalyst behind his family's physical fitness, he's not bothered about losing even one of his own 70-some pounds.

And that's OK.

"If it weren't for Garth, we'd be home sitting on the couch," Rebecca said. "Our desire to give him a better life inspired us to live a better life."

11
Immortal Emmy

It didn't matter that there was a nasty headwind that day on the Chesapeake Bay or that they'd only been paddleboarding a handful of times. Bryan and Camille Smith were having a blast, and so was Emmy. At 80 pounds, the black Lab they nicknamed the "barge queen" crossed her paws and seemed to smile from the nose of Bryan's board, as he struggled to push past the chop. Jokingly, he yelled, "Hey, black dog, paddle!"

The words struck a chord with Camille and marked the beginning of a years-long adventure on the water for this married couple. "That's it! That's it!" Camille screamed. "That's the name of our company!"

Bryan, a longtime whitewater kayak instructor, had seen SUP beginning to take off and couldn't resist Camille's contagious enthusiasm for the sport. Within months, they'd both become SUP instructors and started their business offering paddleboard lessons, tours, and rentals in central Virginia.

Their logo, a simple illustration of Emmy, is a tribute to the sweet Lab, abused, abandoned, and sent to a kill shelter, before being rescued and placed in the Pen Pals Prison Dog Program. As a puppy there, she helped inmates learn patience and trust. And they helped her do the same.

Emmy was 9 months old when Bryan and Camille adopted her. By the time they established Black Dog Paddle, she was 7 but still full of energy. The company's mascot, she's super patient with crowds that gather to pet her silky coat and kids who tug at her floppy black ears.

By now, more than 2,000 people have learned to SUP with Black Dog Paddle. Every paddler becomes an instant "pack member." And every paddler knows Emmy. "Black Dog Paddle introduced her to so many people and she loves all of them," Camille said. "I'm so happy and grateful for the experience. She has been so loved."

12
Waters Less Traveled

The tattoo around Trevor DeHaas' left calf is a permanent reminder that peace is best found when one goes his own way. The music from *Pursuit of Happiness* by hip-hop artist Kid Cudi, Trevor's tattoo is the melody he has chosen to live by. With his beloved dog Kahlua — and an impressive following on Instagram — he's inspiring thousands of others to do the same thing.

At the end of long days, when his 20-something colleagues at a Philadelphia start-up trade cubicles for bar stools, Trevor takes his own route. He heads outdoors with Kahlua, paddleboarding, longboarding, or hiking at sunset. He's the type of guy who would go paddling alone in a snowstorm. And he has.

He'd come with some friends to Marsh Creek Lake near his home in Downingtown, Pennsylvania, that day to rent kayaks. But something else caught his eye. It looked like a surfboard, but he knew that it wasn't. He tried to convince his friends to try one, but when no one would budge, he shelled out $20 and went it alone…once again.

When Trevor found paddleboarding, he found something else — a sense of freedom he'd never known. He was sold. But good gear can be costly, so he pulled a MacGyver, returning to the park with his mom's old windsurfing board and a canoe paddle. It was nowhere near glamorous, but Trevor couldn't have cared less.

"Eventually, I just tossed out the money to get my own board," he said.

He'd been going solo for more than a year before bringing Kahlua along. He'd seen her online and patiently waited for weeks while she was rescued from an Alabama kill shelter and moved to foster care. On the hour-long drive to a PetSmart in Yardley to meet her in person, he felt his heart flutter. The first time he'd laid eyes on her, he'd fallen for her floppy ears and spindly tail, but he couldn't stop thinking about those spectacular spots.

He splurged on a breed test to uncover her heritage – half regal and gentle Great Dane, half Catahoula. Officially called the "Louisiana Catahoula leopard dog," this canine, famous for its unusual spotted coat and piercing eyes, was bred to hunt boar. Now, the only things Kahlua would be hunting with Trevor were outdoor adventures.

"I knew right away I was going to take this dog paddleboarding," he said. "It used to get pretty lonely out on my trips."

First stop: bling. Trevor bought a harness, a collar, a lifejacket, and a bone-shaped dog tag – all in a powdery pink. Then he wasted no time getting Kahlua out on the water, taking her the very next day to paddleboard at the lake where he'd discovered the sport.

Kahlua was nervous at first, but Trevor stayed upbeat, and they worked at it all summer. To make sure she associated the board with fun times, he toted all manner of trinkets and treats to the park. After losing tough-rubber Kongs, and a bevy of balls and bones, to the lakebed – a wasteland of dog toys under the water – he learned to bring items that float. Kahlua was catching on, too.

Trevor started documenting their adventures on Instagram, and people started to notice. His photos – he's posted hundreds of them – have been liked, shared, and "regrammed," even picked up by GoPro.

"I like to inspire people with photos," Trevor said. "Paddling is a great way to bond with your dog. It's so different. It's pretty cool, all the people who reach out [in response to my posts]."

ratherbeodilel: *Want to do that!!!*

darwinsday: *Amazing shot... Made me stop to check out more!*

killdevilfalls: *Your feed is easily one of my favorites. Love the GoPro shots. Seriously think it's about time I invest in one.*

Trevor brought a different type of emotion to his fan base when he took another dog – his mother's miniature golden retriever, Kandy – to the lake.

He posted a picture that day, along with this moving message: *When's the last time you did something for the first time? 15½ years old, and Kandy paddleboarded for her first time ever. We are having Kandy sent to doggy heaven today and I wanted to celebrate her amazing life by taking her to do something she has never done. Gonna miss you, Kandy Kane.*

Emotional responses, like the one from "malelia honu," poured in: *Thank you for sharing this touching photo/story with us. I've been putting off trying paddleboarding, but if Kandy can do it, I bet I can too. Thank you for caring so deeply about your pets.*

Having Kahlua at home helped fill the void Kandy's passing left in Trevor's mom's life. This sweet spotted dog brought them — and thousands of others who follow the duo's adventures online — something else, too, a valuable truth.

"Kahlua has taught me that life can be simpler," Trevor said. "When I'm out on the water with her, all my work, relationship, and monetary problems sink to the bottom of the lake."

photo by Kelsy Gibos

13
A *Second* Second Chance

Kelsy Gibos tugged at the yellow nylon, hammering spikes into the hard ground. Her boyfriend, Travis Johnson, hunted for wood, while she rolled out sleeping bags, plumping two extra-soft spots for the dogs.

"We tried to be normal and do normal things," Kelsy said of the impromptu camping trip. "I knew the next day we'd have to say goodbye, and it could be forever."

Outside, the tent glowed like the sun, a beacon of warmth in the chill of the night. Inside, Kelsy held tight to Travis and their Australian cattle dogs, Twigs and Trout. As she kissed a wet nose and dug her fingers deep into thick fur, one pink tongue licked the tears from her face.

Travis had managed the nearly impossible, tracking down Kelsy in a crag in the Canadian Rockies, where she'd been fighting a wildfire. He'd been desperate to relay the test results from the vet – regarding the blood-stained snow where the dogs had relieved themselves. Kelsy clung to the clunky phone her section chief had handed her. As Travis' voice crackled through the connection, she struggled to hear – and *believe* – what he was saying.

They'd turned their lives topsy-turvy to finally get dogs of their own. Adventure hounds, all four – Kelsy, Travis, Twigs, and Trout – they made a great team. Sledding, hiking, canoeing, and kayaking, they never sat still. Now, huddled in a tent between their home in Alberta and the fast-moving fire Kelsy had to get back to, one life hung in the balance. In the few precious hours they had together, she worked to convince them – and herself – they'd been lucky to love each other, no matter how much time they had left.

photo by Kelsy Gibos

Back in the '90s, while some girls played with pint-sized Polly Pockets and cherished burgeoning Beanie Baby collections, Kelsy was different. "We lived in the mountains," she said. "You grabbed your bike and that was that." As she grew in the quiet town of Blairmore, near Alberta's stony Crowsnest Pass, so did her athletic pursuits. When she wasn't climbing, biking, skiing, or hiking, she practiced another pastime — yearning for a dog.

Each birthday and Christmas, dogs made her wish list. And each birthday and Christmas, that's where they stayed. She begged her parents year after year for a pet, and they'd come through: cats, rabbits, hamsters, and gerbils. Never a dog, though. She could count on getting something about dogs – a book about breeds or a manual on care, their glossy pages filled with Labs and Chihuahuas, hounds and terriers – all of which she longed to hold.

Then that one year, there it was, under the tree. A dog with a collar, a tag, and a leash. She named the plush Pound Puppy "Big Guy" and loved it as much as she could. Ah, if that's all she could have, she would take it.

"I was pretty excited," she said. "Anything 'dog' at that point was a major bonus."

She became a young woman with a life and career of her own before her dog day would come. Even then, though, it would be a difficult decision. When fire pays the bills, you're on call 24/7. A pop-up blaze could send her clear across Canada or even into the U.S. and away from home for weeks.

In 2003, she was 22, fresh from a summer with the Alberta Junior Forest Rangers, where she'd gotten the basics under her belt, when the Lost Creek Fire swept into Crowsnest Pass. When it hovered for weeks, threatening to destroy her family home, firefighting took on a new meaning for Kelsy.

She landed a menial job, counting sticks for the Wildland Fire Operations Research Group, and there was no turning back. "Fire is like a storm," she said. "Once you get in, it's hard to get out."

Now a fire behavior analyst with a master's degree in forestry from the University of Toronto, she gets paid to think like the blaze, get into its head and predict how the weather, the wind, the soil, and the wood – everything – will shape the course of its path. Her work has whisked her across the globe, from Fort Providence and the Northwest Territories of Canada to the Canterbury Plains and Southern Alps of New Zealand. But it was the desert-like plains of Southern Australia and the Black Saturday Fires that led Kelsy and Travis to Twigs and Trout.

Australia's worst-ever bushfire disaster had claimed nearly 200 lives in less than a day. Kelsy would go there to try to understand why.

Travis stayed in Alberta to wait out her six-month assignment, but when months turned into a year and Kelsy kept landing new work in Australia, he left his job to join her. They lived in a few rooms tacked onto the back of a pizza shop in the Alpine Shire town of Myrtleford. Mesmerized by the smell of baked bread and sauce, they feasted on pies fat with tomatoes and herbs grown by the local Italians, and they lived as they pleased.

Free to explore their new homeland, they motorcycled across the dusty terrain, combed the crisp coastline in their Ford Falcon station wagon, hiked national parks. And one other thing. "I was always looking for dogs online," Kelsy said, "following rescue groups."

When she stumbled across four husky and Australian cattle dog puppies at a shelter in Sydney, she grabbed Travis. It was just a few miles away, but by the time they got there, only a brother and sister were left. They were full of worms and covered with fleas, but "so adorable," Kelsy said. They'd foster them, find them good homes. At least that's what she told the shelter staff...and Travis.

Within weeks, they'd revamped their lives. Abandoned their pizza-shop flat for a house with a yard and a fence. Exchanged their Yamaha for an all-purpose pick-up. Made their way through a maze of puppy supplies. And started saving their overtime dollars.

Twigs, named for the kindling Kelsy collected when she first worked in wildfire, was black, the runt of the litter, timid and unsure. Trout, in tribute to Travis' obsession with fly-fishing, was the soft color of ginger, and she was bolder, a boundary-pusher. It was "a typical brother-sister relationship," Kelsy said. "A pain in the butt."

None of it mattered, though. Being a dog owner was all she'd imagined and more, and she pursued her new role with a passion.

"We exposed them to everything when they were puppies," said Kelsy, who turned to the water for basic obedience, using the canoe and the kayak to teach Twigs and Trout to sit and to stay. "We took them on boats. We took them to pubs. We took them into crowds. To musical festivals. On public transit. We took them everywhere."

The dogs joined their drives, hikes, and trips, of course. They kayaked together in sugary coves, swam with sea lions, and capitalized on their natural propensity to pull. They signed up for canicross, skijor, and dog sledding. Competing as "Team TNT," they were unstoppable.

The dogs were 4 when Kelsy's work in the Land Down Under began to run dry. She and Travis considered staying on in Australia, but Canada was calling. It was time to go home. It was a difficult decision; little did they know it would be life saving.

But first they'd have to get themselves – and two 50-pound dogs – across an 80-degree temperature gap, 8,000 miles, and a wide-open ocean. For Kelsy and Travis, the trip would take a few days. For the dogs, who would have to fly separately, it took longer. Kelsy was determined to make the cross-continental trip as seamless as possible.

She'd kept their crates for the plane in the backyard for months, filling them with toys, treats, and relaxing lavender oil, so they'd get used to them. They rented a car and drove eight hours to Sydney to limit the dogs' air travel. They scheduled comfort stops along the way, where Twigs and Trout would get food and baths. And they picked them up in Vancouver so the family could make the 11-hour drive back to Blairmore together.

"They're my most precious belongings," Kelsy said, "so I was ready to do whatever it took."

Back in Victoria, Australia, it was a balmy 77 degrees on that February day when they landed in Canada. In Alberta, the mercury wouldn't budge above zero. Concerned for the dogs, Kelsy and Travis engaged in a flurry of shopping for canine cold-weather gear, including coats, boots, and neck tubes. Mother Nature knew better.

"They grew really thick coats really fast," Kelsy said. "They puffed right up."

Again, Mother Nature was watching out for them. It was a fateful Easter Day storm – and a bathroom break after dinner with Kelsy's parents – that revealed the blood-stained snow. It was Trout.

They made an appointment with the vet. Probably just a urinary tract infection, he said, nothing a round of antibiotics wouldn't fix. He was wrong; after a few treatments, things hadn't cleared up. Healthy and young, Trout had shown no other symptoms, but they scheduled more tests, just in case, including an ultrasound. With Kelsy out of town working a fire, Travis volunteered to take Trout for the follow-up.

That's when the crackly phone call came into base camp. As Kelsy struggled to hear him through the static, Travis laid out the news. An oversized kidney. A huge mass. Probably cancer. Resistant to chemotherapy. Trout needed surgery. Immediately.

"Everything stopped for a moment," Kelsy said. "It was mind-blowing. It was awful."

And the news was about to get worse. If the cancer had spread, Trout might not make it through surgery. Kelsy tried to process the information, her heart racing faster than the flames she'd been fighting. Travis offered to drive the dogs three hours to the nearest town, so Kelsy could see them, and her section chief agreed to release her for the evening. She scrambled into a work truck and raced down the mountain.

Travis parked at a supermarket, watching shoppers stroll in and out with their carts full of groceries, until Kelsy pulled up. He popped the hatch on their sporty Mazda 5, so she could see Twigs and Trout. She couldn't get her hands on them fast enough.

"We sat there together and cried," she said.

At the campsite, the foursome rallied. They went for a walk. Took pictures on the banks of the North Saskatchewan River. Built a fire. Made dinner. Played guitar. And professed their undying love for the dogs, especially Trout. The next day at lunchtime, Kelsy had to leave. The blaze she'd been battling had made its way to the edge of a national park.

"I said goodbye and had to go back to putting wet stuff on hot stuff," she said. "My heart was breaking."

Trout's surgery lasted four hours. She went to sleep with two kidneys and woke up with one. Though they found no sign the cancer had spread, doctors said it probably had. They gave her eight months to live, maybe a year, and urged Kelsy and Travis to limit her physical activity.

It was advice they simply could not abide.

"We can't leave Trout behind," Kelsy said. "We can't lock her in a box, especially when we're not sure how much time she has left. We had things we still needed to show her."

In Australia they were unable to afford a canoe of their own; Kelsy improvised by hitching a kayak to a pontoon boat so they could explore as a family. So for her wedding shower, she'd forgone the typical towels and cutlery sets, asking for a 16-foot Wenonah Aurora, instead. "It really came in handy while Trout was healing," said Kelsy.

They got to work quickly — starting on the water. They lined the hull of their canoe with towels and pads for Trout to lay comfortably. As a group they witnessed sunrises and sets on the water while Trout recovered. "The boat allowed us to be outside together as a family. I think all the fresh air helped Trout heal, especially the calmness of the water, and the wind in her face."

After a full recovery next was hiking, skiing, and boating across the sprawling continent. They posted a "bucket list" online, asked friends for suggestions, and started ticking them off as fast as they could. Trout ate a whole steak. Slept in a king-size bed. Stood on a glacier. Dipped her paws in the other side of the Pacific.

Twigs and Trout even mushed out of the start chute of the famous Yukon Quest dog sled race. And they did something else. They watched Travis and Kelsy get married. They have the pictures — Trout with a flower-ringed collar and turquoise toenails, Twigs in a dapper plaid bowtie — to prove it. Their honeymoon was a scenic canoe trip for four.

More than a year since the surgery, Travis and Kelsy still do a lot of reading and research, and panic when any little thing about Trout seems off. "We live with that regularly," she said, adding that they constantly are aware a terrible disease lurks.

Trout could be completely cancer-free, of course. They really don't know. What they're 100 percent sure of, though, is that this dog, abandoned with her siblings as a puppy, is experiencing a *second* second chance. For better or worse, until death do them part, this family of four is making the most of every minute they have.

"Dogs are awesome. They live purely in the moment. Trout doesn't think about dying or that this might be her last ride. She doesn't care," Kelsy said. "When she's in the boat with us, that's all that matters."

photo by Jen Gardiner

Epilogue

When they're young, they test us. They eat our shoes…and our couches. They leave their hair – and other surprises – throughout our homes. They scratch and lick, wallow in who knows what, and keep running off after that one neighborhood cat.

When they're old, they make us worry. When they start to gray around the muzzle, stop short of that last tennis ball chase, forfeit the bed for the rug at the end of it. That's when they tug at our heartstrings, sometimes forcing us to make unthinkable decisions.

We're dog lovers, though, and we know it's worth it. Our dogs are there when the rest of the world seems to have turned its back on us. They don't care how much money we have in our pockets or when we took our last shower. They are always willing to listen; always ready to celebrate; and always, always happy to see us. They are lovers and tender hearts and sweet things and more.

The journey of writing this book introduced us to people who truly understand all of this, how special dogs are, how their unconditional love for us can help heal our bodies, our minds, and our souls. The people described in the previous pages have made a commitment to their pets, a promise to treat them as they deserve to be treated. With love. With respect. As our friends.

More than that, they've taken that love and companionship to the water and found magic out there. There is something so basic – something supremely cathartic – about the combination of friendship and water. Whether it's in a lake, on a pond, or out in the sea; in a kayak, on a paddleboard, or with fishing rod in hand. When we are on the water alone with our dogs, our best friends – sun beaming down on us – we are at home.

See you on the water!

With Love

Our dogs live much shorter lives than we do. We know this when we get them. We try to ignore that knowledge, but it usually creeps up on us, one way or the other.

In working on this book, we met wonderful dogs — and dog families. One of those dogs was Gertie, a three-legged pit bull who used a custom-made cart to get around. With her perseverance and gentle spirit, Gertie inspired so many on the streets of New York. Even with all she endured, she just kept on pushing.

Sadly, Gertie passed away unexpectedly before the completion of this book. All who loved her were devastated. We tried rewriting the end of her story but decided against it. Thanks to Jens Rasmussen, Kimberly Faith Hickman, and Millie Rasmussen, for sharing Gertie's story and for guiding us in how to handle this sensitive situation.

This book is about the wonderful gifts dogs bring to our lives while they're here, it's about how little they ask in return, it's about the peace and camaraderie we find when we take that friendship into the water. Together, afloat, we are unstoppable.

"Roll on, Gertie girl," Jens posted after her death. "Nothin' gonna stop you now."

Acknowledgements

Anna Billingsley
Words can't express our gratitude for your time and expertise. Thank you for helping us polish this book for dog lovers to enjoy – you're the BEST!

Better SUP Than Sorry | bettersurfthansorry.com
Thank you for donating PUP Decks to many of the pups and paddlers featured in this book.

Ruffwear | ruffwear.com
Thank you for providing Hydro Planes and water toys to each dog featured.

Zuke's | zukes.com
We are very appreciative for the generous bags of treats for each dog featured in the previous pages. Ever wonder how we got the dogs to look so good in the pictures? Our secret is Zuke's!

photo by Norm Shafer

About the Authors

Maria Christina Schultz, outdoor enthusiast, ACA-certified stand up paddleboard instructor, art director, and photographer. Originally from Buffalo, New York, Maria is now based in central Virginia, where she lives with her husband and two Australian shepherds, Riley and Kona. The first day Maria got on a stand up paddleboard, Riley was with her; they learned the sport together. They attracted lots of attention and curiosity from people who wanted to learn to paddle with their own dogs. But with few resources available on training and guidance, Maria took matters into her own hands. She combined her passions for graphic design, photography, and paddling to create her first book, *How to SUP With Your PUP*. Maria also teaches SUP PUP classes in Richmond and other cities along the East Coast. When she's not out paddling with her dogs, Maria enjoys mountain biking, hiking, climbing, skiing, and finding new ways to wear herself – and her dogs – out.

photo by Reza Marvashti

Lisa Chinn Marvashti started her writing and editing career at a daily newspaper in the '90s. She's written about everything from belly-lights and mantyhose – yes, man-ty-hose – to health and the military. Her work has appeared in publications as diverse as *The Denver Post* and *Ride* magazine. When she isn't hauling her kids to soccer (NOT in a minivan) or keeping her husband on task, she likes to spend time with her sweet yellow Labrador, Jackson.